Unless otherwise indicated, all Scripture quotations are taken from the King James Version of the Bible.
"Seeds of Wisdom On Relationships"
ISBN #: 1-56394-081-7 / B-14
Copyright © 2001 by **MIKE MURDOCK**

All publishing rights belong exclusively to Wisdom International.
Publisher/Editor: Dr. Deborah Murdock Johnson
Published by The Wisdom Center.
4051 Denton Hwy. Fort Worth, Texas 76117
1-817-759-BOOK · 1-817-759-2665 · 1-817-759-0300
MikeMurdockBooks.com

1
SEND SOMEONE A SIGNAL THAT THEY MATTER.

❖

☐ *Everyone Needs Reassurance of Their Worth.*

☐ Remind yourself throughout today that each person you meet has encountered waves of criticism, condemnation and inferiority...*you can change this.*

☐ Your words of reassurance can be like water on their Seeds of Hope.

THE WORD

"The Lord God Hath Given Me The Tongue of The Learned, That I Should Know How To Speak A Word In Season To Him That Is Weary."   (Isaiah 50:4)

2

ABANDON ABUSIVE FRIENDSHIPS.

- ☐ There Are 4 Kinds of People In Your Life: Those Who Add, Subtract, Divide And Multiply.

- ☐ *Those Who Do Not Increase You, Inevitably Will Decrease You.*

- ☐ It is the responsibility of others to discern your worth.

Visit My Website..! At WisdomOnline.com

THE WORD

"Make No Friendship With An Angry Man; And With A Furious Man Thou Shalt Not Go: Lest Thou Learn His Ways, And Get A Snare To Thy Soul." (Proverbs 22:24-25)

3

COMPLIMENT SOMEONE TODAY.

☐ A Popular, But Inaccurate Statement Is, "Words Are Cheap." Nothing could be farther from the truth.

☐ Words *cause* wars. Words *settle* wars. Words *create* the waves of emotion that control our world.

☐ Your words of kindness today could easily create the wave that carries someone to their dream.

Buy Books At www.MikeMurdockBooks.com

THE WORD

"Death And Life Are In The Power of The Tongue: And They That Love It Shall Eat The Fruit Thereof." (Proverbs 18:21)

4
CONFIDE IN FEW.

☐ Someone has said that even a fish would not get caught if it kept its mouth *shut!*

☐ Confidentiality is a *gift* to be shared in the privacy of prayer or with an intercessor God has assigned to your life.

☐ Never share your troubles with someone *unqualified* to help you.

THE WORD
"...And Discover Not A Secret To Another: Lest He That Heareth It Put Thee To Shame, And Thine Infamy Turn Not Away."   (Proverbs 25:9-10)

5

CELEBRATE THE OPINIONS OF OTHERS.

☐ One of the greatest gifts you will ever give anyone is...*the Gift of Recognition.*

☐ Every husband... wife... and child... is authorized by the Creator to have a viewpoint, and an opportunity to express it.

☐ *Honor their right to be heard.*

THE WORD

"Let Nothing Be Done Through Strife or Vainglory; But In Lowliness of Mind Let Each Esteem Other Better Than Themselves." (Philippians 2:3)

6
QUENCH THE URGE TO JUDGE.

☐ You cannot draw conclusions as long as there is missing information.

☐ *Things Are Never As They First Appear.* Reserve judgment.

☐ Never attempt to explain...or penalize someone for actions *you* do not fully understand.

Buy Books At www.MikeMurdockBooks.com

THE WORD

"Therefore Thou Art Inexcusable, O Man, Whosoever Thou Art That Judgest: For Wherein Thou Judgest Another, Thou Condemnest Thyself; For Thou That Judgest Doest The Same Things."

(Romans 2:1)

7
MAKE SMILE YOUR STYLE.

☐ Your face *telegraphs* your attitude... toward *life*...toward *others*...about *yourself*.

☐ Your countenance *creates a climate that attracts* people toward you or causes them to move away from you.

☐ When you smile *first*, you have decided the direction the relationship will go.

Buy Books At www.MikeMurdockBooks.com

THE WORD

"Who Is As The Wise Man? And Who Knoweth The Interpretation of A Thing? A Man's Wisdom Maketh His Face To Shine, And The Boldness of His Face Shall Be Changed." (Ecclesiastes 8:1)

8
DEVELOP THE GIFT OF ROMANCE.

———————❧———————

☐ Romance is when you deliberately *create a special moment or memorable event* in someone's life.

☐ Don't wait for your mate to create a perfect occasion. Aggressively, creatively and with spontaneity, start scheduling unique moments and methods to express your love.

☐ To be unforgotten...do something *unforgettable* TODAY.

THE WORD
"For This Cause Shall A Man Leave His Father And Mother, And Shall Be Joined Unto His Wife, And They Two Shall Be One Flesh." (Ephesians 5:31)

9
LEARN SOMETHING "NEW" ABOUT SOMEONE YOU LOVE.

☐ *Knowledge Increases Confidence.* The more knowledgeable you become about someone, the more capable you become at anticipating their needs.

☐ Develop a Personal Portfolio of their particular preferences, such as favorite car, food, colors, songs, books and secret ambitions.

☐ Our Heavenly Father created uniqueness to be discovered, appreciated and *celebrated*.

☐ Greatness will unfold with each discovery.

THE WORD
"And The Lord Make You To Increase And Abound In Love One Toward Another." (1 Thessalonians 3:12)

10
INTERVIEW YOUR CHILDREN.

☐ Your child is worth knowing. *Really* knowing.

☐ Talk. Exchange. Observe. Carefully collect any piece of information that paints a portrait of this "heritage of the Lord."

☐ Communicate with the intent to *learn*, not condemn.

☐ Give your child what he cannot find anywhere else—*non-judgmental conversation*—and he will keep coming back.

THE WORD

"Lo, Children Are An Heritage of The Lord: And The Fruit of The Womb Is His Reward. As Arrows Are In The Hand of A Mighty Man; So Are Children of The Youth. Happy Is The Man That Hath His Quiver Full of Them: They Shall Not Be Ashamed..."
(Psalm 127:3-5)

11
GENERATE ENERGY.

☐ *God Energizes.* In Genesis 1, He created...moved...spoke...divided... called...and so forth.

☐ You are His offspring. *You were created for movement.* Your tongue speaks. Your eyes see. Your ears hear. Your hands grasp. Your feet walk. Even your mind creates thoughts, *each containing a different measure of energy.*

☐ You are a Living Current, carrying others into your future. Use your life today to excite others about the God you serve and the *future made possible* through a commitment to Jesus Christ.

THE WORD
"For In Him We Live, And Move, And Have Our Being." (Acts 17:28)

12
INTERROGATE YOUR FRIENDS.

☐ Everyone Is A Well of Information. *Draw from it.* Drop your bucket regularly into that Well.

☐ Schedule an appointment this week with your 3 most successful friends.

☐ Bring your list of most important questions and *get the answers you need.*

ORDER YOUR COPY TODAY!
"The Uncommon Husband"
(B-211 / 174pg / $15)
817-759-BOOK (2665)

13
FURNISH GENTLENESS.

☐ Gentleness Is Like Heat In A Cold World.

☐ Those around you bear the wounds of Rivalry, Jealousy and Inferiority.

☐ *Pour the Oil of Gentleness* and you will become their greatest memory of the day.

THE WORD

"And The Servant of The Lord Must Not Strive; But Be Gentle Unto All Men, Apt To Teach, Patient."　(2 Timothy 2:24)

14
SOW AFFECTION GENEROUSLY.

☐ Hospital tests have proven that even babies will die if they do not receive touching and loving affection. *You are not an exception.*

☐ Reach out to someone today. *Touch... hug.*

15
INSIST ON INTEGRITY.

☐ Integrity Is *Truthfulness*. It is doing what you say you will do.

☐ *Demand* it from yourself and *reward* it in others.

☐ Do right by others and God will do right by you.

THE WORD
"Be Kindly Affectioned One To Another With Brotherly Love; In Honour Preferring One Another." (Romans 12:10)

16
REPROVE WITH SENSITIVITY.

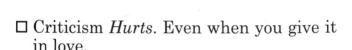

☐ Criticism *Hurts*. Even when you give it in love.

☐ Yet, it is your personal responsibility to provide caution, correction and warnings when someone you love is on the brink of disaster.

☐ Your instruction is their opportunity for *promotion* from God.

THE WORD
"Poverty And Shame Shall Be To Him That Refuseth Instruction: But He That Regardeth Reproof Shall Be Honoured."
(Proverbs 13:18)

17

CELEBRATE THOSE WHO CELEBRATE YOU.

☐ Those Who Discern Your Worth Deserve Special Recognition.

☐ Even Jesus instructed His disciples to respect those who received them and disconnect from those who rejected them.

☐ *Go where your contribution is celebrated.* Jesus did.

THE WORD

"And Into Whatsoever City or Town Ye Shall Enter, Enquire Who In It Is Worthy; And There Abide Till Ye Go Thence. And When Ye Come Into An House, Salute It. And If The House Be Worthy, Let Your Peace Come Upon It: But If It Be Not Worthy, Let Your Peace Return To You." (Matthew 10:11-13)

18
TALK IT OUT.

☐ Friendships Die Through *Neglect*.

☐ Don't expect others to read your mind. *Voice your concerns* over any offense and *express your desire* to make things right.

☐ Silence often waters the Root of Bitterness. TALK IT OUT.

ORDER YOUR COPY TODAY!
"The Gift of Wisdom For Mothers" (B-70 / 32pg / $10)
817-759-BOOK (2665)

19
RESURRECT HOPE IN SOMEONE TODAY.

☐ Hope Is The Expectation of *Favorable Changes.*

☐ Don't permit someone you love to remain depressed and devastated by their present circumstances.

☐ Remind them that Jesus Christ is still the Healer and Miracle-Worker in *every* circumstance of life.

THE WORD

"But Sanctify The Lord God In Your Hearts: And Be Ready Always To Give An Answer To Every Man That Asketh You A Reason of The Hope That Is In You With Meekness And Fear."   (1 Peter 3:15)

20
SKIP WARFARE TODAY.

☐ *Make Today A Peaceable Day.*

☐ Don't feed an argumentative spirit in those around you.

☐ Insist on praying together with those who pursue points of disagreement.

☐ God is well-known for *honoring* peace-makers.

THE WORD
"If It Be Possible, As Much As Lieth In You, Live Peaceably With All Men."

(Romans 12:18)

21
TRIUMPH OVER TRIVIA.

- ☐ *Think of Each Friendship As A Beautiful Flower In The Garden of Your Life.*

- ☐ That Garden must be nurtured, fertilized and watered regularly.

- ☐ Don't let petty and insignificant differences—Trivia—sap the beauty of those flowers.

THE WORD

"Let All Bitterness, And Wrath, And Anger, And Clamour, And Evil Speaking, Be Put Away From You, With All Malice: And Be Ye Kind One To Another, Tenderhearted, Forgiving One Another, Even As God For Christ's Sake Hath Forgiven You."
(Ephesians 4:31-32)

22
SALVAGE SOMEONE.

- □ *You Are Not The Only Person Who Is Struggling Today.* Others around you are hurting, too.

- □ *Be extremely attentive to the silent cries* of someone close to you who may be drowning in the Ocean of Helplessness.

- □ Permit God to make you their Lifejacket.

THE WORD

"Brethren, If A Man Be Overtaken In A Fault, Ye Which Are Spiritual, Restore Such An One In The Spirit of Meekness; Considering Thyself, Lest Thou Also Be Tempted." (Galatians 6:1)

23

NEVER COMPLAIN ABOUT WHAT YOU PERMIT.

☐ *Your Circumstances Are Not Permanent.*

☐ You have permitted your present circumstances or they would not exist.

☐ What you tolerate, you authorize to exist.

☐ Either accept the present without complaint or make a decision *to use your faith* and *attract a miracle* from God.

THE WORD

"Jesus Said Unto Him, If Thou Canst Believe, All Things Are Possible To Him That Believeth."   (Mark 9:23)

24
FERTILIZE FRIENDSHIPS.

☐ Don't permit the name of a friend to be maligned in your presence.

☐ Don't absorb a slanderous report about a friend, unless he is present to defend himself.

☐ A good friend is worth any *price*, any *effort*, any *defense*.

THE WORD

"A Man That Hath Friends Must Shew Himself Friendly: And There Is A Friend That Sticketh Closer Than A Brother."

(Proverbs 18:24)

25
WITHDRAW FROM CONTENTIOUS PEOPLE.

☐ A contentious person is a trouble-maker. He spreads discontent, frustration and distrust.

☐ He gossips. He slanders. He promotes strife.

☐ Do not feed a relationship with such a person.

THE WORD

"As Coals Are To Burning Coals, And Wood To Fire; So Is A Contentious Man To Kindle Strife." (Proverbs 26:21)

26
KEEP YOUR WORD.

☐ Carefully review and fulfill any vows, promises or pledges you have made to anyone.

☐ *Never Promise What You Cannot Produce.*

☐ Make things right with anyone you have wronged in the past.

THE WORD

"A Good Name Is Rather To Be Chosen Than Great Riches, And Loving Favour Rather Than Silver And Gold."

(Proverbs 22:1)

27
RECOGNIZE THAT OTHERS INCREASE YOUR WORTH.

☐ Your *best* qualities will surface in the presence of good people.

☐ Treasure any friend who generates *energy* and *enthusiasm* toward your dreams or goals.

☐ Go the extra mile to nurture and protect any God-given relationship.

THE WORD

"Two Are Better Than One; Because They Have A Good Reward For Their Labour. For If They Fall, The One Will Lift Up His Fellow: But Woe To Him That Is Alone When He Falleth; For He Hath Not Another To Help Him Up."
(Ecclesiastes 4:9-10)

28
MAKE ANGER WORK FOR YOU.

☐ Anger Is Energy. *Harness it*.

☐ Some anger can be devastating to your family, your career or your life. You can *master* it through prayer or channel it into a worthwhile project.

☐ *Direct* your anger towards your true adversary, satan, instead of those you love.

FREE Book Downloads..! At FreeBook.tv

THE WORD
"Be Ye Angry, And Sin Not: Let Not The Sun Go Down Upon Your Wrath: Neither Give Place To The Devil."
(Ephesians 4:26-27)

29
LEARN LOVE-TALK.

☐ Love-Talk Breathes Excitement Into Every Relationship.

☐ Love-Talk is letting another know how much you care...through your words, a gesture or giving of a gift.

☐ Say, "I love you" today...whisper it... shout it...write it in a note...or with a flower—*just say it* to the one you love.

THE WORD
"Many Waters Cannot Quench Love, Neither Can The Floods Drown It."
(Song of Solomon 8:7)

30
BECOME SOMEONE'S BRIDGE.

☐ Someone may open up and share the dream of their heart to you...*listen*.

☐ Someone close to you may ache to hear an approving encouraging word from you...*say it*.

☐ Someone may make a simple request that could unlock an important door for them...*do it*.

ORDER YOUR COPY TODAY!
"The Gift of Wisdom For Achievers" (B-68 / 32pg /$10)
817-759-BOOK (2665)

31
NULLIFY SATANIC ATTACKS AGAINST YOUR FRIENDS.

☐ Your prayers can *cancel* satan's Assignment against your family and friends.

☐ *Call their name* boldly before the throne of God today and *make your request known* in their behalf.

☐ *Expect* your prayer of agreement *to produce* miraculous results, as He promised in His Word.

Visit My Website..! At WisdomOnline.com

THE WORD
"Moreover As For Me, God Forbid That I Should Sin Against The Lord In Ceasing To Pray For You."   (1 Samuel 12:23)

DR. MIKE, I AM RECEIVING JESUS AS MY SAVIOR TODAY..!

I accept Jesus As my Lord and Saviour today for 3 reasons: I need Forgiveness...a Friend...a Future.

"Dear Jesus, I Ask You To Come Into My Life Today, And To Forgive Me For Anything I Have Done That Was Not Good. I Believe That You Died For Me And That You Will Forgive Me When I Do Wrong Things. Thank You For Your Love And Forgiveness. I Love You, Jesus, And I Accept You Now As The King of My Life And The Ruler of My Heart. In Jesus' Name. Amen." Remember to talk to Jesus every day.

ORDER YOUR FREE BOOK TODAY..!

☐ Yes, Mike! I made my decision to receive Christ today. I prayed to Jesus today and asked Him to be the King of my life. Please send me my free gift of your book "31 Keys To A New Beginning" to help me with my new life in Christ.

B14351

Name _____

Address _____

City _____ State _____ Zip_____

Phone _____ E-Mail _____

B14352

☐ Enclosed Is My Seed-Faith Gift of $_____ For Your Ministry..!

☐ Cash ☐ Check ☐ Money Order ☐ Credit Card

Credit Card # _____

Exp. _____ Signature _____

B1435GC

1-844-789-SEED (7333)

Mail To: **The Wisdom Center**
P.O. BOX 1169, Argyle, TX 76226

Write Me A Note..!

☐ Dr. Mike, I Loved This Book, "**Seeds of Wisdom On Relationships**." Here's How It Helped Me:

_____

_____

_____

_____

May I Pray For You..?

☐ Yes, Please Pray For Me And Stand With Me In Agreement For The Following:

_____

_____

_____

_____

_____

_____

B1436GC

"*Again I Say Unto You, That If Two of You Shall Agree On Earth As Touching Any Thing That They Shall Ask, It Shall Be Done For Them of My Father Which Is In Heaven.*" -**Matt. 18:19**

DR. MIKE MURDOCK

1. Has embraced his Assignment to Pursue...Proclaim...and Publish the Wisdom of God to help people achieve their dreams and goals.

2. Preached his first public sermon at the age of 8. Preached his first evangelistic crusade at the age of 15.

3. Began full-time evangelism at the age of 19, which has continued since 1966.

4. Has traveled and spoken to more than 23,000 audiences in over 200 countries, including East and West Africa, Asia, Europe and South America.

5. Noted author of over 900 books, including best sellers, Wisdom for Winning, Dream Seeds, The Double Diamond Principle, The Law of Recognition and The Holy Spirit Handbook.

6. Created the popular Topical Bible series for Businessmen, Mothers, Fathers, Teenagers; The One - Minute Pocket Bible series, and The Uncommon Life series.

7. Has composed thousands of songs such as "I Am Blessed," "You Can Make It," "God Rides On Wings of Love" and "Jesus, Just The Mention of Your Name," recorded by many gospel artists.

8. Is the Founder and Senior Pastor of The Wisdom Center, in Fort Worth, Texas...a Church with International Ministry around the world.

9. Has appeared often on TBN, CBN, BET, Daystar, Inspirational Network, LeSea Broadcasting and other television network programs.

10. Has led over 3,000 to accept the call into full-time ministry.

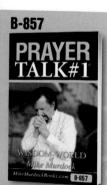

ENCLOSED IS MY SPECIAL SEED OF:

☐ $100, Please Send Me "5001 Wisdom Quotations of Mike Murdock." B14401

☐ $112, Please Send Me "The Millionaire's Bible." B14402

☐ $200, Please Send Me "Millionaire100 Library" Tablet. *(100 e-Books)* B14403

☐ $500, Please Send "The Mike Murdock Library 500" Tablet. *(Over 500 e-Books)* B14404

☐ $1000, Please Send My Gifts. *(The Millionaire 100 Library, The Mike Murdock Library 500, The Wisdom Bible, 5,001 Wisdom Quotations of Mike Murdock.)* B14405

METHOD OF PAYMENT

☐ AMEX ☐ DISCOVER ☐ MASTERCARD
☐ VISA ☐ CHECK ☐ MONEY ORDER
☐ CASH Or Call **1-844-789-SEED** (7333)

NAME ON CARD_____

CARD# _____ - _____ - _____ - _____

EXP. DATE _____/_____ TOTAL ENCLOSED $_____

SIGNATURE _____

E-MAIL_____

B1440GC